A Note From Denise Renner

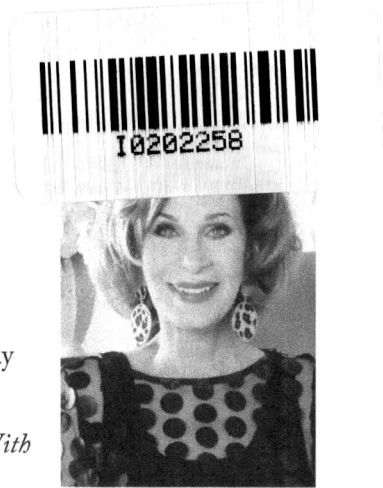

The Word of God is so powerful in our lives. It is essential that every person spend time with God and study His Word in order to stay spiritually strong in these last days.

This study guide corresponds to my *TIME With Denise Renner* TV program by the same title that can be viewed at **deniserenner.org**. My desire is that through these lessons, you find the encouragement and freedom in Christ that you need. I believe the Holy Spirit is going to speak to you through the words you read in this study tool and that as you begin to use it, you will be *propelled* into the abundant life God has planned for you. I encourage you to make the effort to receive all He has for you and all He wants to do in you — it will definitely be worth it!

Whether you have walked with the Lord a long time or have just begun to follow Him, there is so much He wants to give you from His Word. He sees where you are, and He wants to meet you there.

> Therefore do not worry about tomorrow, for tomorrow
> will worry about its own things.
> Sufficient for the day is its own trouble.
> Matthew 6:34

Your sister and friend in Jesus Christ,

Denise Renner

How the Presence of God Changes You

Copyright © 2022 by Denise Renner
1814 W. Tacoma St.
Broken Arrow, Oklahoma 74012

Published by Rick Renner Ministries
www.renner.org

ISBN 13: 978-1-6675-0310-3

eBook ISBN 13: 978-1-6675-0311-0

TOPIC

Can God Change Your Identity?

SCRIPTURES

1. **Judges 6:11-27** — Now the Angel of the Lord came and sat under
   the terebinth tree which was in Ophrah, which belonged to Joash
   the Abiezrite, while his son Gideon threshed wheat in the winepress,
   in order to hide it from the Midianites. And the Angel of the Lord
   appeared to him, and said to him, "The Lord is with you, you mighty
   man of valor!"

   Gideon said to Him, "O my lord, if the Lord is with us, why then
   has all this happened to us? And where are all His miracles which
   our fathers told us about, saying, 'Did not the Lord bring us up from
   Egypt?' But now the Lord has forsaken us and delivered us into the
   hands of the Midianites."

   Then the Lord turned to him and said, "Go in this might of yours,
   and you shall save Israel from the hand of the Midianites. Have I not
   sent you?"

   So he said to Him, "O my Lord, how can I save Israel? Indeed my
   clan is the weakest in Manasseh, and I am the least in my father's
   house."

   And the Lord said to him, "Surely I will be with you, and you shall
   defeat the Midianites as one man."

   Then he said to Him, "If now I have found favor in Your sight, then
   show me a sign that it is You who talk with me. Do not depart from
   here, I pray, until I come to You and bring out my offering and set it
   before You."

   And He said, "I will wait until you come back."

   So Gideon went in and prepared a young goat, and unleavened bread
   from an ephah of flour. The meat he put in a basket, and he put the
   broth in a pot; and he brought them out to Him under the terebinth
   tree and presented them. The Angel of God said to him, "Take the
   meat and the unleavened bread and lay them on this rock, and pour
   out the broth." And he did so.

Then the Angel of the Lord put out the end of the staff that was in His hand, and touched the meat and the unleavened bread; and fire rose out of the rock and consumed the meat and the unleavened bread. And the Angel of the Lord departed out of his sight.

Now Gideon perceived that He was the Angel of the Lord. So Gideon said, "Alas, O Lord God! For I have seen the Angel of the Lord face to face."

Then the Lord said to him, "Peace be with you; do not fear, you shall not die." So Gideon built an altar there to the Lord, and called it The-Lord-Is-Peace. To this day it is still in Ophrah of the Abiezrites.

Now it came to pass the same night that the Lord said to him, "Take your father's young bull, the second bull of seven years old, and tear down the altar of Baal that your father has, and cut down the wooden image that is beside it; and build an altar to the Lord your God on top of this rock in the proper arrangement, and take the second bull and offer a burnt sacrifice with the wood of the image which you shall cut down." So Gideon took ten men from among his servants and did as the Lord had said to him. But because he feared his father's household and the men of the city too much to do it by day, he did it by night.

SYNOPSIS

The five lessons in this study on *How the Presence of God Changes You* will focus on the following topics:

- Can God Change Your Identity?
- God Shows Up Best in Emergency Situations
- You Can't Experience God's Presence and Remain the Same
- Rahab — An Encouragement for Our Faith
- God's Presence Is Your Identity-Changer

The emphasis of this lesson:

One encounter with God's presence can supernaturally change your life! When you experience the presence of God, you can receive a new identity, a new assignment, and new power for your call. It doesn't matter what others have called or labeled you — when you come into agreement with the Spirit of God and receive His call, your identity is

changed. You can go forth in your assignment with a fresh impartation of peace and power from the Lord Jesus!

Throughout the Old Testament, the Angel of the Lord appeared to certain individuals, bringing a particular message or piece of instruction to them. This was a dramatic visitation that marked these people for life. God's presence changed their identity, gave them an assignment, and imparted power unto them for the task at hand. One person who experienced such an encounter with the Angel of the Lord was Gideon. Judges 6 records this remarkable story and demonstrates how God's presence changed Gideon's identity from a fearful, timid man to a mighty man of valor. It also reveals how the Lord gave Gideon an assignment and empowered him for his calling.

The Presence of God Brings Healing

Denise shared a wonderful testimony from a viewer who was recently healed during a previous *TIME With Denise Renner* broadcast. The woman wrote, "I was diagnosed with a spur on my left foot. I could not walk at all, and it even got worse after therapy. But yesterday, I watched your program *TIME With Denise Renner*. When you were talking about God's presence, I immediately felt it. When the program finished and I stood up, I walked easily. I began to praise, dance, and sing."

This healing testimony highlights the power of the presence of God. When we enter God's presence, every good thing is released. God's power meets us where we are and answers whatever need we may have. In the case of this viewer, her greatest need was to receive healing in her foot. When she entered God's presence by listening to the teaching of the Word, God's power reached out to her at that moment and healed her foot. She went forth healed and whole, totally changed by the presence of God.

God's Presence Personified

All throughout the Bible, we find references to the presence of the Lord. In the Old Testament, we see God's presence manifested in the ark of the covenant, the pillar of fire, and the cloud by day. We also see God's presence being personified in an unusual way through the Angel of the Lord. In fact, Scripture records several instances where the Angel of the Lord appeared to different individuals bringing an important message or word of encouragement.

Many people have often wondered about the exact identity of the Angel of the Lord. Scholars believe He is readily identified with the Lord God and is a distinct person from God the Father. After the birth of Christ in the New Testament, the Angel of the Lord no longer appears, leaving many to believe He is indeed an attribution to Jesus Christ Himself in the Old Testament.

Whenever the Angel of the Lord (or we could say Jesus) visited people in early Bible days, it marked them for life as they came face to face with God's presence in a tangible, personal way. Throughout this study, we will look at three specific people in the Old Testament who experienced a visitation from the Angel of the Lord: Gideon, Hagar, and Jacob. Each of these individuals were completely changed from that one encounter, and they went forth with a new identity, a new assignment, and fresh power to do what God had called them to do.

The Angel of the Lord Visits Gideon

Gideon's story begins in Judges chapter 6. During this time, the Israelites were in a backslidden state and had turned to worshiping false gods. As a result of their disobedience to God, they were suffering greatly from the hands of the Midianites. In fact, the Midianites were so mean to them that they were constantly destroying all their livestock and produce, leaving the Israelites in a continual state of poverty, hunger, fear, and lack. Because of the Midianites' endless plundering and perpetual violence against them, the Israelites were even forced to hide themselves in caves away from the grasp of their enemies!

It is in this historical context that we find Gideon, a young man who was threshing wheat by the winepress as he attempted to hide his produce from the greedy hands of the Midianites. From all appearances, Gideon wasn't brave or strong or even someone with remarkable abilities. He was just an ordinary person who was trying to survive by staying out of the sight of his enemies.

However, Gideon's life was about to change completely with one encounter from the Angel of the Lord. This visitation begins in Judges 6:11 and 12: "Now the Angel of the Lord came and sat under the terebinth tree which was in Ophrah, which belonged to Joash the Abiezrite, while his son Gideon threshed wheat in the winepress, in order to hide it from the

Midianites. And the Angel of the Lord appeared to him, and said to him, 'The Lord is with you, you mighty man of valor!'"

Of course, you can imagine Gideon's confusion and bewilderment at this visitor's announcement. Here he was hiding from his enemies in the winepress — he probably felt like anything but a mighty man of valor!

Understandably, Gideon immediately began arguing with the Angel of the Lord. He replied, "…O my lord, if the Lord is with us, why then has all this happened to us? And where are all His miracles which our fathers told us about, saying, 'Did not the Lord bring us up from Egypt?' But now the Lord has forsaken us and delivered us into the hands of the Midianites" (Judges 6:13).

Like Gideon, we can sometimes find ourselves arguing with the Lord when His call comes to us. We may say, "Lord, we don't have the money to do that. We can't do what You asked us to do." However, God is so compassionate toward us even in our weakness. Just because we argue with Him at first doesn't mean He stops talking to us.

In Gideon's case, the Angel of the Lord continued to talk with him, giving him further instructions and answering his questions: "…Go in this might of yours, and you shall save Israel from the hand of the Midianites. Have I not sent you? …And the Lord said to him, 'Surely I will be with you, and you shall defeat the Midianites as one man.'" (Judges 6:14,16).

When Gideon first encountered the Angel of the Lord, his immediate response was to argue with Him and bring up all the reasons why the call of God wouldn't work. Gideon even brought up the fact that he felt incapable of such a call — he was the least of his father's clan and his clan was the weakest in Manasseh. However, none of these arguments from Gideon changed God's mind about him or the call He had placed on his life. Rather, the Angel of the Lord continued to affirm and supernaturally confirm Gideon's identity and assignment until Gideon finally surrendered to the call, accepted his new identity, and believed the Lord would be with him in his assignment (see Judges 6:16-21).

God Reveals Identity in His Presence

The powerful story of Gideon teaches us an important truth about what happens when we come into the presence of God. When Gideon was visited by the Angel of the Lord, he had a hard time believing what the

Angel was telling him. His identity was wrapped up in weakness and in the insignificance of his tribe. However, when he encountered the presence of God, a new identity was released unto him, and he was supernaturally changed from a timid, fearful young man into a *mighty man of valor*!

Like Gideon, we may believe something very different about ourselves that's not actually true. But when we enter the presence of God, He reveals another identity to us. He tells us who we are in Him, how He sees us, and what He's called us to do. He equips us with power and anointing to execute our assignment, and He promises to be with us every step of the way.

It's so important to listen to God when He calls us. It's easy to say, "Lord, I can't do this. I'm not smart enough. I'm too weak for this assignment. I'm nobody special." However, when God calls us, He confers a new identity upon us. He tells us, "Yes, you can do this assignment. You're not the weak. You're not the timid. You're not the stupid. You're not unqualified. You are the one I chose. You're the one that's anointed for this task. You're the one that's after My heart. I see your difficulties, but I am with you, and you will make it through this. You will conquer this!"

It's time for us as the Body of Christ to step up into our place and listen to the Holy Ghost. We must listen to His assignments! And when we listen to Him, He will tell us, "I know the devil might be telling you who you are, but that's not who you are. Your past might be telling you who you are, but that's not who you are either. Even those with a degree of authority in your life might be telling you who you are, but that is NOT your identity. *I'M telling you who you are!* You are more than a conqueror through Christ Jesus. THIS is your identity!"

The most important thing we can ever do is to agree with the Holy Spirit. When He challenges us to let go of previous labels that have held us back, we need to obey. We need to come into agreement with Him and see ourselves as He sees us. We need to accept His identity as the truth in our lives.

God Releases Peace in His Presence

After this visitation ended, it dawned on Gideon that he had been speaking with the Angel of the Lord. At this revelation, Gideon said, "...Alas, O Lord God! For I have seen the Angel of the Lord face to face" (Judges 6:22). In that instant, God spoke to him and released His supernatural peace, saying, "…Peace be with you; do not fear, you shall not die" (Judges 6:23). In response to this, Gideon built an altar there to the Lord and called it *The Lord is Peace.*

When the Lord speaks to us about something and we submit to Him, He will always leave us with His peace. *Any time* we encounter God's presence, His peace is released to us. His peace is the great enabler. Once we stop arguing with God and yield to His call, His peace will come to us. His peace will even quiet our soul from arguing with Him! And when His peace comes, we are in the right place to receive His power.

God Releases Power in His Presence

Gideon's story continues in Judges 6:25-27 with God commanding him to tear down the altars of Baal that his father had built. Now this was a huge task! To be obedient to God's voice, Gideon was going to have to go against the opinions and traditions of his own father. Can you imagine how much boldness this required? This wasn't something Gideon could do in his own strength; he had to be empowered by God to do such a thing.

Of course, this act of obedience didn't come without some difficulty. After Gideon obeyed and tore down those altars, people wanted to kill him! But God was faithful to deliver him, just as He had promised.

Similarly, we may encounter challenges when we set out to obey God. We may even face great opposition from others like Gideon experienced. But no matter how difficult the road of obedience may become, we can rest assured that God will be with us in our assignment. The Bible says tells us that no enemy is bigger than God. Romans 8:31 says, "…If God is for us, who can be against us?"

Think about this for a moment — the Bible tells us that even at the end of the age when the Antichrist appears, Jesus will destroy him with just one word from His mouth (*see* 2 Thessalonians 2:8). The Lord is not intimidated by the Antichrist or any other enemy because *He is the Lord of hosts.* He is the Lord of the armies of Heaven. He is the Lord Almighty! He is the One who stands with us to do what we thought was impossible.

When we understand the power of God's presence, it will change us forever. We may have a small opinion of ourselves and our own abilities, but in God's presence, He can speak to us and remind us of His calling, His strength, and His anointing. He can release His peace to us whenever we are overwhelmed with the task at hand. He can also give us the power to do something that seems too hard to accomplish in our own strength.

The next time we come into God's presence and the Holy Spirit tugs at our hearts regarding God's plan for our lives, let's remember the story of Gideon. While we may feel inadequate for our assignment, God tells us, "I have called you. You are not who others say you are. You are who I say you are. You can do it. I am with you."

As we accept God's call and His identity, His presence can change us right where we are. We can align our hearts and mouths with what He is saying to us. We can come into agreement with Him and say, "Yes, Lord, I can. I can do all things through Christ who strengthens me. I receive my assignment, and I will obey because You are with me every step of the way."

STUDY QUESTIONS

Be diligent to present yourself approved to God, a worker who does not need to be ashamed, rightly dividing the word of truth.
— 2 Timothy 2:15

1. In the story of Gideon, what three things were released to him when he encountered the Angel of the Lord?
2. Do you think Gideon would have had the courage to obey the command to tear down the altars that his father built if he had not encountered the presence of God?
3. Go back and read Judges chapter 6 during your own Bible study time. What do you see as evidence of an outward change in Gideon's behavior once he encountered the presence of God?

PRACTICAL APPLICATION

But be doers of the word, and not hearers only, deceiving yourselves.
— James 1:22

1. What labels, words, or perceptions from others have you allowed to shape your identity about yourself? How is God challenging you to see yourself differently according to what He has called you?

2. Have you been afraid to obey God because you may face opposition from others? What Scriptures are you standing on to come against fear and timidity?

3. Think about the assignment God is giving you. Write down what you see yourself doing in obedience to your calling. How many lives can be affected by your obedience? What lives could be affected if you didn't obey God?

TOPIC

God Shows Up Best in Emergency Situations

SCRIPTURES

1. **Genesis 16:4-14** — So he went in to Hagar, and she conceived. And when she saw that she had conceived, her mistress became despised in her eyes.

   Then Sarai said to Abram, "My wrong be upon you! I gave my maid into your embrace; and when she saw that she had conceived, I became despised in her eyes. The Lord judge between you and me."

   So Abram said to Sarai, "Indeed your maid is in your hand; do to her as you please." And when Sarai dealt harshly with her, she fled from her presence.

   Now the Angel of the Lord found her by a spring of water in the wilderness, by the spring on the way to Shur. And He said, "Hagar, Sarai's maid, where have you come from, and where are you going?"

   She said, "I am fleeing from the presence of my mistress Sarai."

   The Angel of the Lord said to her, "Return to your mistress, and submit yourself under her hand." Then the Angel of the Lord said to her, "I will multiply your descendants exceedingly, so that they shall not be counted for multitude." And the Angel of the Lord said to her:

   "Behold, you are with child, and you shall bear a son. You shall call his name Ishmael, because the Lord has heard your affliction. He shall be a wild man; his hand shall be against every man, and every man's hand against him. And he shall dwell in the presence of all his brethren."

Then she called the name of the Lord who spoke to her, You-Are-the-God-Who-Sees; for she said, "Have I also here seen Him who sees me?" Therefore the well was called Beer Lahai Roi; observe, it is between Kadesh and Bered.

2. **Proverbs 30:21-23** — For three things the earth is perturbed, yes, for four it cannot bear up: for a servant when he reigns, a fool when he is filled with food, a hateful woman when she is married, and a maidservant who succeeds her mistress.

3. **Isaiah 53:4** — Surely He has borne our griefs and carried our sorrows; yet we esteemed Him stricken, smitten by God, and afflicted.

SYNOPSIS

In the Bible, God's presence often shows up in emergency situations, leaving people changed, strengthened, and empowered. One such person who experienced God's presence during a crisis was an Egyptian slave woman named Hagar, whose story takes place in Genesis 16. While alone, pregnant, and on the run, Hagar encountered the Angel of the Lord in the middle of the wilderness. After this supernatural event, the Lord changed her identity, gave her a promise for the future, and revealed His great compassion to her.

The emphasis of this lesson:

God's presence can meet you in the middle of a crisis! No matter what others have done to you, you can rest assured that God hears your cries and sees you in your affliction. When you experience the presence of God, you can receive a new identity, healing, power, and a promise. God is faithful and compassionate toward you, and He has the power to deliver you from every emergency.

The Power of God's Presence

As we continue our study on the presence of God, we are reminded how God's presence can touch every part of our life. In fact, when we received the new birth, it was God's presence that changed us. In our sinful state, He found us and picked us up. His grace and mercy came upon us and changed us into another person. We received the miraculous touch of God the moment salvation came to us, and we have never been the same since. His presence is powerful indeed!

Hagar: A Woman Who Experienced the Presence of God

The Bible records some unique instances when the presence of God touched the most unlikely people. Some of these situations were what we would even consider emergencies. These were events that were extremely difficult and required God's compassionate touch and divine rescue for those involved.

One such person who experienced God's presence in the middle of a crisis was an Egyptian slave woman named Hagar, whose story takes place in Genesis 16. At this time, Abram and Sarai were waiting for God's promise of a son. However, Sarai grew impatient in the process and decided to take matters into her own hands. Thinking she could inherit God's promise another way, she suggested to her husband that their son could be born through her maidservant Hagar instead. So, Sarai offered Hagar to Abram, he slept with her, and Hagar conceived.

Of course, this plan backfired on Sarai once Hagar became pregnant. The Bible tells us that Sarai became "despised" in the eyes of her maidservant because she herself couldn't conceive. This reminds us of what Proverbs 30:21-23 says: "For three things the earth is perturbed, yes, for four it cannot bear up: for a servant when he reigns, a fool when he is filled with food, a hateful woman when she is married, and a maidservant who succeeds her mistress."

As tensions in Abram's house increased, Sarai began to deal harshly with Hagar. We do not know exactly what that means — perhaps she beat her, embarrassed her, screamed at her, put heavy burdens on her, or took some other form of disciplinary action. In any case, the situation was so bad that Hagar chose to flee from Sarai and escape this hurtful environment. This crisis in Hagar's life led her to the wilderness — and that is exactly where she encountered the presence of God.

The Angel of the Lord Appeared to Hagar

Genesis 16:7 says, "Now the Angel of the Lord found her by a spring of water in the wilderness, by the spring on the way to Shur." As we saw in the story of Gideon, the Angel of the Lord can be interpreted as Jesus Christ in the Old Testament. It was this same Angel of the Lord that was looking for Hagar and appeared to her in the middle of her crisis. While Hagar wasn't seeking God, He was looking for her. His compassionate heart was searching for this lost one, and He found her in her suffering.

When the Angel of the Lord appeared to Hagar, He addressed her by name, asking her where she was coming from and where she was going. Hagar replied, "...I am fleeing from the presence of my mistress Sarai" (Genesis 16:8). Then the Angel of the Lord said something surprising to her: "...Return to your mistress, and submit yourself under her hand. ...I will multiply your descendants exceedingly, so that they shall not be counted for multitude. ...Behold, you are with child, and you shall bear a son. You shall call his name Ishmael, because the Lord has heard your affliction." (Genesis 16:9-11).

Although Hagar had gone through an emotionally and physically difficult experience, God still had a plan and promise for her. This moment in the presence of God completely changed her identity and her future. While she had come into this encounter as a pregnant Egyptian slave girl, she was leaving as a mother of a nation because the Lord had compassion on her. He reached out to her, touched her life, and she went forth from that place, never the same again.

The Lord Heard Her Affliction

When the Angel of the Lord visited Hagar, He was aware of her situation, her pain, and her affliction. In fact, He said to her, "...The Lord has heard your affliction" (Genesis 16:11). Her cries and anguish didn't go unnoticed by Him. He saw everything that had transpired in her situation, including how Sarai had dealt so harshly with her. He heard her affliction and was moved with compassion toward her.

This reminds us of what Isaiah 53:4 says, "Surely He has borne our griefs and carried our sorrows; yet we esteemed Him stricken, smitten by God, and afflicted." Jesus was afflicted by God so that we would be delivered from those who afflict us. Our affliction was nailed to the Cross and paid for by the blood of Jesus.

The Bible says that God heard Hagar's affliction. What happened to her wasn't her fault, but because of her station in life, she didn't have the power to stop it. However, Hagar's cries didn't go unnoticed by God. He heard her affliction and stepped into her moment of crisis to change her and empower her.

Whenever we encounter a difficulty in life or come into a place of affliction, we can be encouraged by Hagar's story. Not only does Jesus hear our affliction, but He paid the price for it at the Cross. We can take our affliction to Him, and the power of God can deliver us from it and set us free.

The God Who Sees

As Hagar's visitation with the Angel of the Lord came to an end, Genesis 16:13 records this: "Then she called the name of the Lord who spoke to her, You-Are-the-God-Who-Sees; for she said, 'Have I also here seen Him who sees me?'" Hagar had a revelation of the compassion of God — He is the One who sees us in the midst of our suffering and affliction.

Because God is the same yesterday, today, and forever, the compassion that He showed Hagar in the Old Testament is the same compassion that He shows us today. God sees our affliction and hears our cries. He wants to heal broken hearts, deliver us, and bring change into our lives.

Like Hagar, we may be in a difficult situation. Perhaps others have an advantage over us, and we feel powerless to escape. Regardless of the circumstances, if we'll turn to God, He can deliver us! He is the glory and the lifter of our head. He's the One who causes us to throw our shoulders back and say, "I'm not the beaten down. I'm not the one that always loses. I'm trusting in Jesus because I'm more than a conqueror through Him! He lives in me, and I can do all things through Christ who strengthens me."

Whenever God's presence comes on the scene, His power is manifested. He sees us in every difficult, painful circumstance. Perhaps our parents rejected us. Maybe our fathers or mothers abandoned or abused us. No matter what others have done to us, God sees our affliction.

In our state of emergency, we can simply come into God's presence and receive His power into our lives. And just like Hagar, we can experience one moment with the Lord and be changed forever. We can receive God's new identity for us, His deliverance from our affliction, and His promise for our future!

STUDY QUESTIONS

**Be diligent to present yourself approved to God, a worker
who does not need to be ashamed, rightly dividing the word of truth.
— 2 Timothy 2:15**

1. Put yourself in Hagar's shoes for a moment as she was escaping from her mistress. What thoughts might have been going through your mind? How would you have felt? What would you have done?

2. Think about Sarai in this situation. How did her impatience in God's process affect her and those around her?

3. In Genesis 16:8-13, we see how the Angel of the Lord paid special attention to Hagar and her situation. If you were Hagar, how would this personal, compassionate encounter with the Lord affect you?

PRACTICAL APPLICATION

**But be doers of the word,
and not hearers only, deceiving yourselves.
— James 1:22**

1. What is your response to affliction? What do you do when you are hurt by others? Do you take the pain to Jesus, or do you cover it up and try to hide it from Him?

2. What emergency have you been in where you experienced God's compassionate intervention? How did His love and mercy change you?

3. Take a moment to think about a time when you were secretly hurt by someone who had authority or power over you. Perhaps it was a parent, a teacher, or even a pastor. Did you take that hurt to Jesus? Did you call out to Him for His help? How did He help you forgive that person?

TOPIC

You Can't Experience God's Presence and Remain the Same

SCRIPTURES

1. **2 Corinthians 3:18** — But we all, with unveiled face, beholding as in a mirror the glory of the Lord, are being transformed into the same image from glory to glory, just as by the Spirit of the Lord.

2. **Genesis 27:40,41** — "By your sword you shall live, and you shall serve your brother; and it shall come to pass, when you become restless, that you shall break his yoke from your neck."

   So Esau hated Jacob because of the blessing with which his father blessed him, and Esau said in his heart, "The days of mourning for my father are at hand; then I will kill my brother Jacob."

3. **Genesis 32:6-12** — Then the messengers returned to Jacob, saying, "We came to your brother Esau, and he also is coming to meet you, and four hundred men are with him." So Jacob was greatly afraid and distressed; and he divided the people that were with him, and the flocks and herds and camels, into two companies. And he said, "If Esau comes to the one company and attacks it, then the other company which is left will escape."

   Then Jacob said, "O God of my father Abraham and God of my father Isaac, the Lord who said to me, 'Return to your country and to your family, and I will deal well with you': I am not worthy of the least of all the mercies and of all the truth which You have shown Your servant; for I crossed over this Jordan with my staff, and now I have become two companies. Deliver me, I pray, from the hand of my brother, from the hand of Esau; for I fear him, lest he come and attack me and the mother with the children. For You said, 'I will surely treat you well, and make your descendants as the sand of the sea, which cannot be numbered for multitude.'"

4. **Genesis 32:24-30** — Then Jacob was left alone; and a Man wrestled with him until the breaking of day. Now when He saw that He did not prevail against him, He touched the socket of his hip; and the

socket of Jacob's hip was out of joint as He wrestled with him. And He said, "Let Me go, for the day breaks."

But he said, "I will not let You go unless You bless me!" So He said to him, "What is your name?" He said, "Jacob." And He said, "Your name shall no longer be called Jacob, but Israel; for you have struggled with God and with men, and have prevailed."

Then Jacob asked, saying, "Tell me Your name, I pray." And He said, "Why is it that you ask about My name?" And He blessed him there. So Jacob called the name of the place Peniel: "For I have seen God face to face, and my life is preserved."

5. **Genesis 33:4** — But Esau ran to meet him, and embraced him, and fell on his neck and kissed him, and they wept.

SYNOPSIS

An encounter with the presence of God will never leave anyone the same. A wonderful example of someone from the Old Testament who left completely changed by the presence of God is Jacob, whose story is covered in Genesis 27-33. Although Jacob was a deceiver and stole his own brother's birthright, God still had a plan for his life. Jacob's actions eventually caused him to be the target of his brother's wrath, and in a moment of desperation, Jacob prayed to God for deliverance. This prayer eventually led to a wrestling match with God in the middle of the night! That one encounter in God's presence changed Jacob's identity and resulted in a blessing that saved his life.

The emphasis of this lesson:

God's presence will not leave you the same! If you're in danger or trouble, God has a rescue plan for you. By taking time to seek His face, you can encounter God in a whole new way that leaves you changed forever. In His presence, you can find a new identity, deliverance, and restoration. God's blessings are available to you when you encounter His presence!

God's Presence Doesn't Leave Us the Same

As we continue our study on God's presence, we are reminded that when we take time to experience His presence, we never come out the same again. We simply can't be around God and remain the same. Joy replaces sadness. Love dispels hatred. Hope moves in where hopelessness was. God's presence is filled with *every good thing*. Whatever we need from Him to be strong in these last days, we can receive from the Lord in His presence.

Second Corinthians 3:18 tells us, "But we all, with unveiled face, beholding as in a mirror the glory of the Lord, are being transformed into the same image from glory to glory, just as by the Spirit of the Lord." When we look into the Word of God, it's like peering into a mirror — and the reflection looking back at us is not our face but God's. By spending time with Him and meditating on His Word, His life begins to reflect in us. It shows up in our heart, in our attitude, in our patience, and in our faith. Everything God is and has is reflected to us and within us when we come into His presence because His presence changes us!

Jacob: A Deceiver and a Runaway

In Genesis 27-33, we find a powerful example of a colorful character who was changed in the presence of God — and that person is Jacob. As the younger of Isaac's two sons, Jacob was not the inheritor of his father's birthright. That blessing traditionally belonged to his elder brother, Esau. However, Jacob was a deceiver, and he ultimately stole the blessing from his brother by tricking his father into giving the birthright to him! Of course, this resulted in unpleasant circumstances for Jacob as his brother pledged to take revenge and kill him.

Forced to flee his brother's wrath, Jacob moved far away and lived with an extended relative named Laban. There he fell in love with Laban's daughter Rachel, but in order to marry her, Jacob had to work for Laban for seven years. After he fulfilled this seven-year requirement, Jacob was finally able to marry the love of his life. But there was an unexpected twist — Laban deceived Jacob and gave his elder daughter Leah to be Jacob's bride instead. Disappointed, Jacob agreed to work another seven years in order to earn Rachel's hand in marriage.

Finally, after many years of waiting and hard labor, Jacob married Rachel. Over time, both Leah and Rachel gave birth to children causing Jacob's two households to grow considerably. Jacob had also become quite wealthy, accumulating several livestock and servants. It was at this point in his life when he decided to pack up his family and wealth and leave

Laban. Unfortunately, Jacob's brother Esau was still waiting for him with the same vengeful promise to take his life.

Jacob's Prayer

Jacob's story picks back up in Genesis 32. At this point, Jacob was severely afraid because the last thing he had heard all those years ago was that his brother was planning to kill him. And to make matters worse, Jacob's messengers reported Esau was coming to meet him with 400 men. Realizing his dangerous predicament, Jacob went to the Lord in prayer. And as he was praying, Jacob reminded the Lord of a promise He had made to him: "...O God of my father Abraham and God of my father Isaac, the Lord who said to me, 'Return to your country and to your family, and I will deal well with you'" (Genesis 32:9). In the middle of this terrible mess, Jacob reminded God of His promise to take care of him.

When we're facing something terrible, we can follow Jacob's example in our own prayer time. No matter what danger may be surrounding us, we can remind God what He has promised us in His Word. We could be facing any type of difficult situation — a broken relationship, bankruptcy, job loss, sickness — but God is right there to watch over us and see us through the hardship. He will fulfill His Word, and He will take care of us!

The Bible also records another important element of Jacob's prayer in this chapter — his thankfulness. In verse 10, Jacob took time to acknowledge the blessings of God. When he first came into that far away land, he was a single man fleeing for his life. By the time he was returning home, he was married and had a huge family, servants, and wealth. Although he was facing a dangerous situation, Jacob didn't take these blessings for granted.

Jacob's example here shows us that thanksgiving is another important aspect of our prayer life. It's always good to stop and remember God's goodness to us. We might experience some very difficult times, but without God's blessings in our life, where would we be? Whenever we're in distress, it's important to get our eyes on Jesus and express our thankfulness to Him.

Jacob ended his prayer with his petition: "Deliver me, I pray, from the hand of my brother, from the hand of Esau..." (Genesis 32:11). Jacob was clear with God in his prayer — he needed deliverance!

Similarly, when we need help from God, we can simply ask Him, and He will hear us. We can remind Him of His promises to meet our needs, heal our bodies, and preserve us in dangerous times. Because the Bible says God will never leave us or forsake us, we can rest in His presence, knowing His rescue is always available to us.

Jacob's Life-Changing Encounter With the Lord

Later that same evening after Jacob prayed, he had an unusual face-to-face encounter with the Lord (*see* Genesis 32:24-30). In fact, the Bible tells us that Jacob "wrestled" with Him all night long! Jacob was in such a serious, desperate situation that he refused to release the Lord until He blessed him. Finally, in verse 28, the Lord said, "…Your name shall no longer be called Jacob, but Israel; for you have struggled with God and with men, and have prevailed." Verse 29 goes on to say, "…And He blessed him there."

What a powerful moment! In this passage, we see that this one encounter with God's presence completely transformed Jacob's identity and his future. Not only did the Lord change his name from Jacob to Israel, but He also answered his prayers by releasing a blessing on him that broke the enmity between him and Esau. The next morning when Jacob rose, he saw Esau far off. But instead of attacking him, Esau "…ran to meet him, and embraced him, and fell on his neck and kissed him…" (Genesis 33:4). The Lord even supernaturally restored the relationship between the two brothers!

We can receive the same kind of miraculous deliverance and restoration that Jacob experienced in his life just by staying in God's presence. We can open our heart to God and tell Him exactly what our problems are. He will listen to us, and He has a plan to save us! It doesn't matter how desperate we are or what troubles surround us. We can go to the Lord in faith and receive His mercy, grace, and help in our time of need.

Just one moment in God's presence can change us. He'll give us a new identity, deliver us, rescue us, and bless us. We can remind God of His promises and express our thankfulness to Him. We can be honest with Him and let Him know exactly what we need. We can stay resolute in our position, refusing to move until we see the answer to our prayer. And if we'll take time to be in His presence, we will begin to see God's reflection in us and experience His delivering power!

STUDY QUESTIONS

**Be diligent to present yourself approved to God, a worker
who does not need to be ashamed, rightly dividing the word of truth.
— 2 Timothy 2:15**

1. How do you see the law of sowing and reaping at work in Jacob's life? Do you think if Jacob hadn't deceived Esau then perhaps Laban wouldn't have tricked him with Rachel and Leah?
2. While Jacob had his share of faults, God still wanted to rescue him. Can you think of other people in the Bible who weren't perfect but who were also rescued by God?
3. In the end of Jacob's story, he experienced supernatural restoration in his relationship with his brother Esau. What other Bible stories come to your mind that feature restoration in relationships?

PRACTICAL APPLICATION

**But be doers of the word,
and not hearers only, deceiving yourselves.
— James 1:22**

1. Have you ever been in a dangerous situation like Jacob where you were threatened? How did you turn to God for help in that situation? How did He rescue you?
2. How often do you give thanks to God in your prayer time? Do you thank Him often, or do you take His blessings for granted?
3. What relationships in your life need to be restored? Take a moment right now and ask God to mend those broken relationships.

TOPIC

Rahab — An Encouragement for Our Faith

SCRIPTURES

1. **2 Corinthians 3:18** — But we all, with unveiled face, beholding as in a mirror the glory of the Lord, are being transformed into the same image from glory to glory, just as by the Spirit of the Lord.

2. **Joshua 2:4-11** — Then the woman took the two men and hid them. So she said, "Yes, the men came to me, but I did not know where they were from. And it happened as the gate was being shut, when it was dark, that the men went out. Where the men went I do not know; pursue them quickly, for you may overtake them." (But she had brought them up to the roof and hidden them with the stalks of flax, which she had laid in order on the roof.) Then the men pursued them by the road to the Jordan, to the fords. And as soon as those who pursued them had gone out, they shut the gate.

   Now before they lay down, she came up to them on the roof, and said to the men: "I know that the Lord has given you the land, that the terror of you has fallen on us, and that all the inhabitants of the land are fainthearted because of you. For we have heard how the Lord dried up the water of the Red Sea for you when you came out of Egypt, and what you did to the two kings of the Amorites who were on the other side of the Jordan, Sihon and Og, whom you utterly destroyed. And as soon as we heard these things, our hearts melted; neither did there remain any more courage in anyone because of you, for the Lord your God, He is God in heaven above and on earth beneath."

3. **Hebrews 11:31** — By faith the harlot Rahab did not perish with those who did not believe, when she had received the spies with peace.

4. **1 Peter 5:7** — Casting all your care upon Him, for He cares for you.

SYNOPSIS

Faith in God can come just by hearing testimonies of God's mighty power. A marvelous example of an Old Testament Bible character who was changed simply by hearing about God's supernatural power is Rahab the Harlot (*see* Joshua 2). Although Rahab had a sinful past, her belief in God led her in a whole new direction! Because of her faith-filled actions, Rahab's life was spared when her city was conquered by the Israelites. Eventually, she married an Israelite and became part of the lineage of Jesus.

The emphasis of this lesson:

No matter what kind of past you've experienced, God can change you from the inside out and give you a new purpose in life. When you take time to hear about the wonderful love and power of God, faith will rise in your heart. You can then step out in faith with your actions because you've placed your trust in the Lord.

Rahab the Harlot

As we continue our study on the presence of God, let's look at another example from the Old Testament of someone whose life was drastically changed by God. This time, our Bible story features a woman who had a bad reputation. Her name was Rahab, and she was a prostitute from the city of Jericho.

Rahab's story is told in Joshua chapter 2. At this point in time, the children of Israel were planning a siege on Jericho. But before they took over the city, they sent two spies into Jericho to spy out the land and gather intel. While the spies were on their mission, they lodged at the house of Rahab the harlot. The king of Jericho eventually discovered the spies were there and sent word to Rahab to bring the men to him. Instead of submitting to the king's request and turning the spies in, she hid them on the roof of her house and told the king's men they had already left Jericho.

Once the king's men had left, Rahab went up to her roof and pulled the spies out of hiding. When she greeted them, she said, "…I know that the Lord has given you the land, that the terror of you has fallen on us, and that all the inhabitants of the land are fainthearted because of you. For we have heard how the Lord dried up the water of the Red Sea for you when you came out of Egypt, and what you did to the two kings of the

Amorites who were on the other side of the Jordan, Sihon and Og, whom you utterly destroyed. And as soon as we heard these things, our hearts melted; neither did there remain any more courage in anyone because of you, for the Lord your God, He is God in heaven above and on earth beneath" (Joshua 2:9-11).

While Rahab did not personally see any of the miracles God performed for the Israelites, she had heard plenty about them! The news of God's power surrounding Israel had spread far and wide, inspiring both awe and fear in the people of Jericho. This reputation of God's presence caused Rahab to recognize that something was indeed different about the God the Israelites served.

Rahab was so touched by hearing about Israel's God that it moved her to a place of faith and action. She acknowledged what she had heard to be true and believed this God was the true God. At the risk of being a traitor to her country and putting her own life in jeopardy, she chose to protect the Israelite spies. Her faith in God caused her to put her trust in Him.

In return for her help, the spies struck an agreement with Rahab — she was to leave a scarlet cord dangling outside her window, and anyone who was with her in that house would be spared when the Israelites came to conquer the land.

Rahab's Faith Changed Her Life

The spies eventually went on their way back to the Israelites' camp to give a report of their mission. Not long after, the Israelites marched on the city of Jericho to lay siege upon the city. As promised, Rahab left a scarlet cord hanging from her window as a sign of protection for her and her family.

Not only did Rahab's faith in God save her life, but it also preserved the lives of those in her household. Furthermore, Rahab's actions changed the course of her life forever. She went on to marry one of the spies who had lodged with her and became the mother of Boaz, who eventually became the great-grandfather of David. Because of her faith in God and a willingness to put her faith into action, this former prostitute became part of the lineage of Jesus.

Rahab's Example of Faith

Despite her questionable beginnings, Rahab is considered a mighty woman of faith in the Bible. In fact, she is recognized in the Hall of Faith in Hebrews chapter 11: "By faith the harlot Rahab did not perish with those who did not believe, when she had received the spies with peace" (v. 31). She's even mentioned in the book of James for her actions of faith.

Rahab's faith is a wonderful example for us in our everyday life. No matter what circumstances may be facing us, we can refuse to worry and put our trust in God. First Peter 5:7 admonishes us to cast all our care upon the Lord because He cares for us, and that's exactly what Rahab did. Even if we find ourselves in an impossible situation, we can choose to turn our eyes to God and be full of faith.

Every time we read the Bible, we see God working miracles for those who have called upon His name. Like Rahab, we have also heard of God's mighty power and supernatural acts. If a harlot who wasn't even part of God's covenant at the time could hear stories about God that caused her to believe in Him, then we can certainly trust our Heavenly Father.

It's time to lay down every heavy load we're carrying. We don't have to lose any more sleep from worry or anxiety. God loves us, and He has the answer to every problem we could ever face. We can take a lesson from Rahab and allow God to deliver us, change us, and reroute our destiny!

STUDY QUESTIONS

Be diligent to present yourself approved to God, a worker who does not need to be ashamed, rightly dividing the word of truth.
— 2 Timothy 2:15

1. Imagine you were Rahab for a minute. What thoughts might have been going through your mind as you risked your life for the Hebrew spies?
2. When the Israelites came in to conquer Jericho, Rahab and everyone living with her was spared. What might her perspective have been of the walls falling all around her while at the same time being supernaturally protected?

3. Rahab's actions of faith led to her changed future. What steps of faith have you taken that have led you down God's path for your life? Where would you be had you not acted in faith?

PRACTICAL APPLICATION

**But be doers of the word,
and not hearers only, deceiving yourselves.
— James 1:22**

1. Although Rahab had a bad past, God changed her and gave her a new life. How is your life different since you became born again? What attitudes and behaviors did you have before you met Christ that you do not have any more?
2. Because Rahab heard about God's power, she believed in Him. What did you hear about God that led you to believe in Him?
3. Are you struggling with depression, worry, or anxiety? If you are, take a moment to release those to God. He cares for you, and He has the power to deliver you from all your troubles.

LESSON 5

TOPIC

God's Presence Is Your Identity-Changer

SCRIPTURES

1. **2 Corinthians 3:18** — But we all, with unveiled face, beholding as in a mirror the glory of the Lord, are being transformed into the same image from glory to glory, just as by the Spirit of the Lord.

SYNOPSIS

Anytime a person encounters God, he is changed. In this review lesson, we recount the stories of Gideon, Hagar, Jacob, and Rahab and recall how God transformed their lives in a moment of time. Although they were from different backgrounds and had their own unique situations, they all had something in common. God touched their life, changed their identity, gave them a new assignment, and gave them the power they needed to accomplish His plan.

The emphasis of this lesson:

The Bible teaches that God's power can change people into the image of Jesus. By spending time in God's presence, studying His Word, and fellowshipping with Him, you can be transformed from the inside out. You can receive a new identity in Christ, a God-given assignment, and supernatural strength. God's presence can change you from glory to glory!

Transformed Into the Image of Jesus

Any time we spend time with the Lord, His power changes us. The Bible says in Second Corinthians 3:18: "But we all, with unveiled face, beholding as in a mirror the glory of the Lord, are being transformed into the same image from glory to glory, just as by the Spirit of the Lord." Whenever we look into the mirror of God's Word, His image is reflected to us. His peace and joy are released to us. His wisdom comes into our hearts, and His plan is made visible to our spirits. We may come into His presence one way, but we will not leave the same. In the presence of God, we are transformed into the image of Jesus!

Spending time with God gives Him an opportunity to speak to us. And in that secret place, God changes our identity, gives us an assignment, and gives us the power to carry out that assignment. While we're looking at Him, He's changing us from glory to glory.

It's critical, therefore, to spend as much time with the Lord as we can. The more we are with Him in prayer, in the study of His Word, in worship, and in sharing Jesus with others, the more His nature is formed within us. His victory becomes a reality in our lives as we continue to be with Him in His presence.

What Gideon, Hagar, Jacob, and Rahab All Had in Common

Throughout this study, we've been looking at the lives of four important people in the Old Testament: Gideon, Hagar, Jacob, and Rahab. They all came from different backgrounds and encountered different types of difficulties in their lives. Two of them were men, and two were women. One was an Egyptian, and one was from Jericho. One was timid, one was a deceiver, one was a servant, and one was a prostitute. While each person had a unique story, this one thing they all had in common: *They were changed by the presence of God.*

Let's remember Gideon's story — he saw himself as a man from the weakest tribe and the least important in his family. But God saw him as a man of valor and might. When Gideon encountered God's presence, it changed both his identity and his assignment. From that point on, Gideon possessed courage, strength, and boldness that he hadn't had before, and God used him mightily to liberate his nation from the hands of the enemy.

In Hagar's story, we were reminded of God's compassion to see us in our affliction. Hagar was a pregnant woman who was treated harshly by those in authority over her. While fleeing from the pain and trauma of her situation, she was visited by the Angel of the Lord. This encounter changed her identity and gave her a promise for the future. When Hagar saw the Lord, her life was altered as she recognized God's mercy and care. She left the wilderness with a promise from God and became the mother of a nation.

As we recount Jacob's story, we understand that he sowed some bad seeds in his life. He was a deceiver and a trickster, and he became afraid because his actions were about to catch up with him. But on the night before Esau, his brother, planned to attack him, Jacob prayed to God for deliverance. This eventually led to a wrestling match with the Lord in which Jacob refused to let go until he was blessed by God, and as a result of this encounter with God's presence, Jacob's name was changed. He went from being seen as a deceiver to being seen as a prince in the eyes of God and man. Not only did he experience God's deliverance from death and destruction, but Jacob was also restored to a healthy relationship with his brother.

Finally, we remember the story of Rahab the harlot. Although she had a questionable past, she believed in God when she heard about His mighty acts for the children of Israel. Her faith in God led her to take action, and she risked her own life to save the Hebrew spies from the king. In response to her just actions, God delivered her and her entire family from being taken down with the city of Jericho. Eventually, she married into the

Jewish nation and became part of the lineage of Jesus. Rahab's testimony of faith became so powerful that her story is honored in the Hall of Faith in Hebrews 11.

In all these situations, God's presence was demonstrated in such a powerful way that it changed identities, restored hope, gave encouragement, imparted strength, delivered from death, brought restoration, and birthed new assignments. If these things happened in the Old Testament for each of these men and women, how much more can we expect to be changed by the power of God when we enter His presence today?

Changed From Glory to Glory

Whenever we feel hopeless, we can run into God's presence and receive His hope and vision for our future. When we are at our worst, God still sees something valuable in us. We may not think we have the confidence to complete a task given to us, but God is there with us, ready to impart strength and power to us.

If we have a past that we're ashamed of, we can run and ask the Lord for forgiveness. Perhaps we've mistreated others — God can change our nature and bring restoration to our relationships. We may not see a bright future in front of us, but God does. If we will go to the Lord, He can show us His glorious plan for our lives.

We are not the rejected or the despised, and we are not alone. We are *more than conquerors* through Him that loved us. We are not without hope, for Jesus is our hope! Despite what our circumstances may look like, we are not defeated. We are not inadequate. God's victory is our victory. His strength is our strength. His provision is our provision. Whatever we have need of, we can find if we will come into God's presence and receive it from Him.

By spending time with God, we can be changed from one place in life to another. We can go from glory to glory as we allow God's Word to soften our hearts and form Christ in us. As we pray, study the Bible, worship God, and gather with other believers, God begins to do a supernatural work in our hearts and among us as the Body of Christ. We are no longer the same as we were before because God's presence supernaturally changes us from glory to glory.

STUDY QUESTIONS

**Be diligent to present yourself approved to God, a worker
who does not need to be ashamed, rightly dividing the word of truth.
— 2 Timothy 2:15**

1. Second Corinthians 3:18 says, "But we all, with unveiled face, beholding as in a mirror the glory of the Lord, are being transformed into
   the same image from glory to glory, just as by the Spirit of the Lord."
   Reading the Bible is critical to our spiritual growth and transforma-
   tion. What other passages of scripture do you know that admonish
   us to meditate on or study God's Word? What are the benefits of
   studying the Bible?

2. In this series, we examined the lives of four people in the Old Testament who were changed by the presence of God. What other people
   from the Bible can you think of who were transformed by the power
   of God?

3. Of all four examples we have studied in this series, which one impacted
   you the most? Which one do you relate to the most and why?

PRACTICAL APPLICATION

**But be doers of the word,
and not hearers only, deceiving yourselves.
— James 1:22**

1. Hebrews 11 is often referred to as the Hall of Faith. Take some
   time today to study that chapter. What other Bible characters are
   mentioned in this chapter that exemplify a life of faith? If you're not
   familiar with some of their stories, make it a point to read the passages of scripture where their lives are mentioned.

2. In your Bible reading this week, what has the Lord been speaking
   to you about specifically? How are you being changed from glory to
   glory by spending time in His Word?

3. As we learned in our study, God can change our identity, give us a
   new assignment, and give us the strength to fulfill that assignment
   whenever we encounter the presence of God. In what ways has God
   changed your identity? What new assignment has He given you?
   How have you been strengthened or empowered to accomplish His
   plan for your life?

Notes

Notes

CLAIM YOUR FREE RESOURCE!

As a way of introducing you further to the teaching ministry of Rick Renner, we would like to send you free of charge his teaching CD, "How To Receive a Miraculous Touch From God."

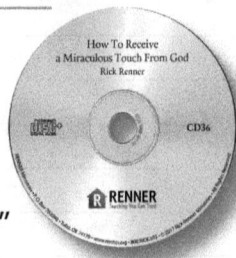

In His earthly ministry, Jesus commonly healed *all* who were sick of *all* their diseases. In this profound message, learn about the manifold dimensions of Christ's wisdom, goodness, power, and love toward all humanity who came to Him in faith with their needs.

☑ **YES, I want to receive Rick Renner's monthly teaching letter!**

Simply scan the QR code to claim this resource or go to: **renner.org/claim-your-free-offer**

Connect WITH US!